First Edition 2003
Second Impression 2006
Paperback Edition 2006

HOOPOE

Published by Hoopoe Books,
a division of The Institute for the Study of Human Knowledge

**Visit www.hoopoekids.com
for a complete list of Hoopoe titles, CDs, DVDs,
an introduction on the use of Teaching-Stories™
and parent/teacher guides.**

ISBN 1-883536-30-8

Library of Congress Cataloging-in-Publication Data

Shah, Idries, 1924-
    The man with bad manners / by Idries Shah ; illustrated by Rose Mary Santiago.-- 1st ed.
        p. cm.
    Summary: A clever boy and other villagers devise a plan to improve the manners of one
of their neighbors. Based on a folktale from Afghanistan.
    ISBN 1-883536-30-8 (hardcover)
    [1. Folklore--Afghanistan.] I. Santiago, Rose Mary, ill. II. Title.

PZ8.1.S47Man 2003
398.2--dc21
[E]
                                                                        2003050816

The Man with Bad Manners

Written by

Idries Shah

HOOPOE BOOKS

BOSTON

ONCE UPON A TIME, many many years ago, when birds flew upside-down, there was a village.

Everyone who had a house in the village also had a field. And in their fields they grew potatoes and carrots and cabbages and all kinds of other crops.

Now, all the people who lived in the village were very courteous and well-behaved, except for one man who had very bad manners.

Whenever anybody said "good morning" to the man
with bad manners, he would say "blah, blah, blah."
And when anybody said "good evening" to him, he
would say "blee, blee, blee."

The people would become annoyed when
he did this, and they would say,
"Why do you have such
bad manners?"

But he would just say, "blah, blah, blah."
Except, of course, when he said, "blee, blee, blee."

For a long time, the people weren't too bothered by the man's behavior. They knew good manners from bad manners, and most of the time they didn't take much notice of the man with bad manners.

But one day he got worse. He began to go out at night and stand outside different houses, and he would beat tin cans and make terrible noises.

BANG! BANG! BANG!

This would wake the people up, and they would lean out of their windows and say, "Why are you making such a racket?"

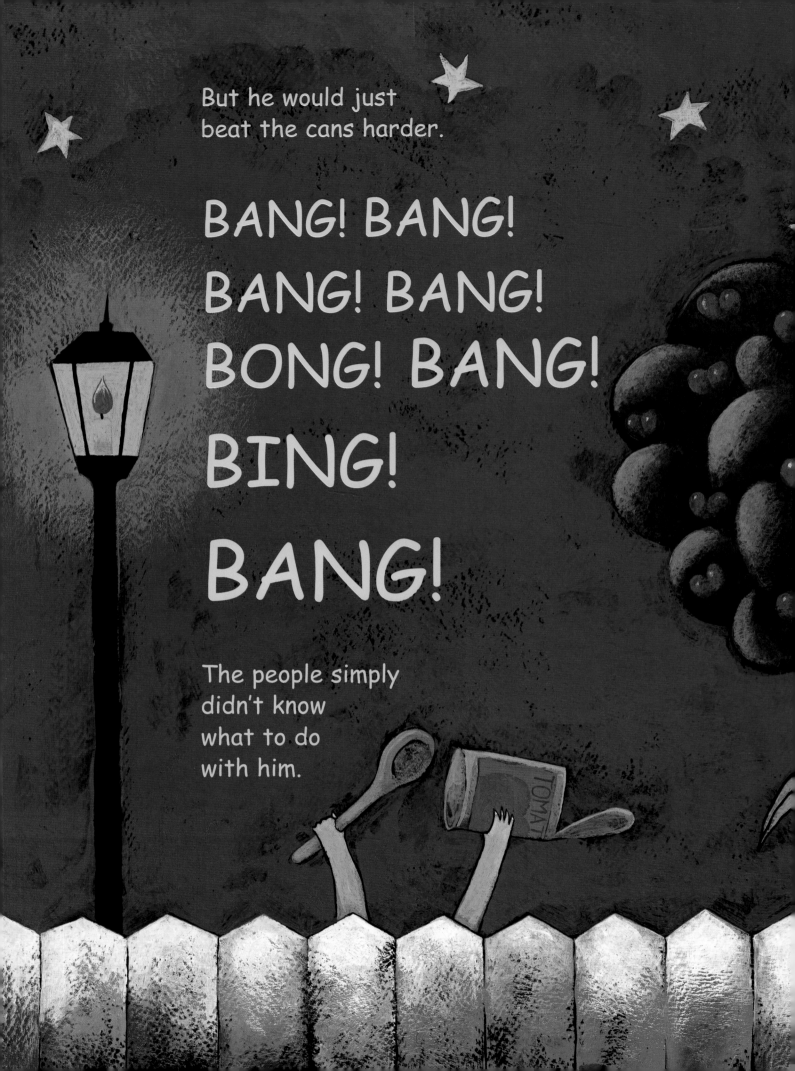

But he would just
beat the cans harder.

BANG! BANG!
BANG! BANG!
BONG! BANG!

BING!

BANG!

The people simply
didn't know
what to do
with him.

Now, one day, the man with the bad manners went to stay with some friends in another village. The people were so glad he was going away that they all gathered to watch him walk out of town.

Among those watching was a very clever boy.

As soon as the man was out of sight, the clever boy stood on a box and called all the people to come together.

And when the people had gathered, the clever boy said, "I want to talk to you about the man with bad manners."

"What a relief!"

"Why should we talk about him?"

"You're right," said the old woman. "He's going to come back, and then he will just annoy us all over again!"

"But he's going to come back!" said the clever boy.

"Yes, indeed," said an old man.

"What can we do?" cried the people.

"I have an idea," said the clever boy. "I've thought of a way to make him change his ways."

"Tell us, quickly!" shouted the people.

"Well," said the clever boy, "the man has a field, and in his field he is growing potatoes. While he's away, we'll take the potatoes out and put carrots in their place.

Then, when he comes back, we can pretend that
it isn't his field and that this isn't even his village."

"What about his house?" asked the old woman.
"He'll go to his house, and he'll know that this is his
village because he'll see his house right there."

"His house is red," said the clever boy. "We'll paint
it green so he'll think it's some other house."

"What if he goes inside?"
asked the old woman.

"I've thought of that, too," said the clever boy.

"We'll paint the walls a different color, and we'll paint the furniture a different color, and then we'll rearrange it. He's sure to think then that it's somebody else's house."

"What good will that do?" several people said.

"Well," said the clever boy, "he'll either go away or he'll change his ways."

"You know," said the old woman, "it just may work!"

And so the people got together and worked very hard. They dug up all the man's potatoes and put carrots in the ground in their place.

They painted the walls outside his house.

They painted the walls inside his house. They painted all the furniture. And they rearranged everything so that it all looked quite different.

Not long afterwards, the man with the bad manners came back. As he walked into the village, he said "blah, blah, blah" and "blee, blee, blee" to everyone he saw, and he hit tin cans just as loudly as ever. Bang! Bang! Bang!

The people gathered around him, and the clever boy said, "Hello there! Who are you?"

"You know who I am," said the man with bad manners, banging on a can.

"Oh, no, we don't!" said the people.

"Yes, you do! This is my potato field," said the man, pointing to his field.

"But there are carrots in this field," said the clever boy, pulling a carrot out of the ground. "This can't be your field."

"But my house is right over there!" said the man.

"What color is your house?" asked the clever boy.

"You know perfectly well that my house is red," said the man.

"But this house is green," said the clever boy.

The man looked carefully at his house and said, "Good heavens! That house is green."

And then he ran over to the window and looked inside and saw that everything was quite unfamiliar.

"Dear me!" said the man, scratching his head. "Maybe I don't come from this village after all."

He looked around at all the villagers, and then looked down at the ground, and all of a sudden, he became very sad. "But, if I don't come from this village, where do I come from?"

"It's a secret," said the clever boy, "but we can tell you the secret only on one condition. You must promise to use good manners and speak courteously and behave properly from now on. If you promise that, we'll tell you the secret."

"I promise! I promise!" said the man. "Please tell me!"

And then the people all spoke at once. "We painted your house on the outside." "We put carrots in your field." "We painted it on the inside." "We painted all your furniture." "And, then, we rearranged it."

"We did it all to teach you a lesson," said the clever boy. "But now that you have promised to behave yourself, we'll change everything back, and we can all live happily ever after."

So, the man with bad manners promised again to change his ways. He promised, and he promised, and he promised. And then the people changed everything back for him.

From then on, when anyone said, "Good morning," to the man, he replied cheerily, "Good morning to you!"

And when anyone said, "Good evening," to the man, he replied courteously, "Good evening to you!"

And he never banged another can ... ever. And so, indeed, everyone did live happily ever after.

Other Books by Idries Shah

For Young Readers
The Clever Boy and the Terrible, Dangerous Animal
The Silly Chicken
The Boy Without a Name
The Old Woman and the Eagle
The Man and the Fox
The Man with Bad Manners
Neem the Half-Boy
The Farmer's Wife
The Lion Who Saw Himself in the Water
Fatima the Spinner and the Tent
The Magic Horse
World Tales
El León que se Vio en el Agua/The Lion Who Saw Himself in the Water
El hombre y el zorro
El hombre maleducado
La Esposa del Granjero/The Farmer's Wife
El Pollo Bobo/The Silly Chicken
El muchachito listo y el terrbile y peligroso animal/
The Clever Boy and the Terrible, Dangerous Animal

Literature
The Hundred Tales of Wisdom
A Perfumed Scorpion
Caravan of Dreams
Wisdom of the Idiots
The Magic Monastery
The Dermis Probe

Novel
Kara Kush

Humor
The Exploits of the Incomparable Mulla Nasrudin
The Pleasantries of the Incredible Mulla Nasrudin
The Subtleties of the Inimitable Mulla Nasrudin
The World of Nasrudin
Special Illumination

Human Thought
Learning How to Learn
The Elephant in the Dark
Thinkers of the East
Reflections
A Veiled Gazelle
Seeker After Truth

Sufi Studies
The Sufis
The Way of the Sufi
Tales of the Dervishes
The Book of the Book
Neglected Aspects of Sufi Study
The Commanding Self
Knowing How to Know